Abbeys of Yorkshire
by Colin Platt

Copyright © English Heritage 1988
First published by English Heritage 1988

Edited by Katy Carter
Designed by Thumb Design Partnership
Printed in England by Litho-Tech, London
c350   3/88

ISBN 1 85074 199 9

Cover illustrations
Front cover, from top, left to right: Whitby Abbey;
Fountains Abbey; monks building (British
Library Add MS 39943, f.39); monk of St Mary's
Abbey, York (Bodleian Library MS Bodley 39,
f.1r).
Back cover: St John of Bridlington (British Library
MS Royal 2A. XVIII, f.7v); Egglestone Abbey;
Rievaulx Abbey; abbot of St Mary's, York
(Bodleian Library, as above).
Inside covers: Pattern based on floor tiles from the
church at Rievaulx Abbey.

▶ **St Cuthbert of Lindisfarne (634–87),
from a twelfth-century wall painting at
Durham Cathedral.** (Dean and Chapter of
Durham)

Introduction

Sweep Yorkshire clean of the Industrial Revolution, and what remains is a landscape fit for monks. Skies are larger in Yorkshire, confrontations with nature more direct than in the South. This is territory for grappling with the Deity. Here men of religion once swarmed like bees. 'A fly and a friar', so the medieval proverb went, 'will fall in every dish'. Few in the county, from the Central Middle Ages, were without a monk or a nun as near neighbour.

But the circumstances were not as elsewhere. Yorkshire, unlike the South, underwent its conversion to Christianity in two distinct episodes: first in the seventh century and then in the eleventh, separated by the irruption of the Vikings. Yorkshire monasticism, swept away in the interval, was almost entirely second wave. It had another quality very much its own. Little remained, even in the tenth and eleventh centuries, of the religious communities of Christian Northumbria. Nevertheless, their memory had been kept alive in the pages of Bede's widely-read *Ecclesiastical History*, an Anglo-Saxon 'best-seller' which remained a continuous inspiration to northern monasticism, and which was almost equally influential in the South. St Wilfrid of Ripon (633–709), memorialised by Bede, left his mark in a cult which spread throughout England from that base; St Hilda of Whitby (614–80), another Northumbrian, still has her devotees to this day. The very Englishness of these northern saints, among whom St Cuthbert of Lindisfarne (634–87) became pre-eminent, was one of the props of national pride through all the humiliations of the Norman

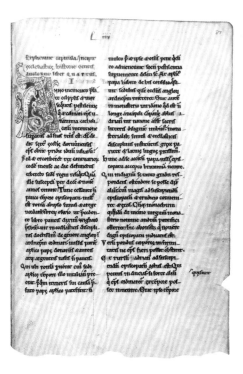

▲ The Venerable Bede's *Ecclesiastical History* told the story of Northumbria's Christian settlement in the seventh and eighth centuries, before the Viking raids. It was widely read in the South also, and was a major influence in the post-Conquest re-settlement of the ancient holy places, beginning with the Mission to the North in the 1070s. (Twelfth-century northern manuscript, Bodleian Library)

◄ St Hilda (614–80), founder of the double monastery (both monks and nuns) at Whitby, was one of Anglo-Saxon England's best-loved saints. Celebrated by Bede, she was known especially for her zeal for learning, for her wisdom, and for her strict adherence to the Rule of St Benedict, banishing private property from her abbey. (Christ Church, Oxford)

Conquest. Yorkshire's second monastic settlement was accomplished by their grace, even if many of its flavours were imported.

It is the character of that settlement which is our theme. We begin with the story of a post-Conquest Benedictine revival, launched by the Northern Mission of the late 1070s, then bending to successive winds of change. Yorkshire, we shall see, because of this late start, was never a major Benedictine province. The Cluniacs scarcely came here, and few of the conquerors' homeland monasteries – very unlike the South – assembled estates or other interests in the county. Yet, from early in the twelfth century, when the bruises of the Conquest had faded and Duke William's 'harrying of the North' had been forgotten, neglected Yorkshire came into its own. Land was plentiful and donors ready to welcome communities generally acknowledged to be the best. First to arrive were the Augustinians – known as 'black canons' from the colour of their robes. Next came the Cistercians, St Bernard's huge 'white monk' army, with the Gilbertines and the 'white canons' (Premonstratensians) close behind. The first houses of nuns are known from the 1130s, and the friars had started settling a century later. Last to establish themselves were the solitary Carthusians, washed up on a tide of late-medieval spirituality which had surged on the back of the Black Death.

This great Christian host, brutally cut down in the 1530s, has left Yorkshire a graveyard of its relics. But the 'bare ruin'd choirs', in Shakespeare's phrase, are no dry bones. Blending austerity of spirit with human fallibility, they have lessons to teach us even now.

▲ Only the skeleton of Whitby's great abbey church now remains. It dates to the thirteenth and fourteenth centuries, when Whitby's monks, assisted by pilgrim offerings at Hilda's shrine, began an ambitious rebuilding. The new choir and presbytery (*right*), laid out by Abbot Roger in the 1220s, more than doubled the size of an already large Anglo-Norman building. This had itself taken the place of the cells, of varying sizes and random plan, in which Hilda's monks had lived. The cells, not now visible, were uncovered by excavation in the 1920s in the area north of the nave of the later church.

Benedictine Yorkshire

In southern and central England, the wealthiest monastic houses were usually those of Anglo-Saxon origin, which had accumulated great estates before the Conquest. Loosely called 'Benedictine' and later known as 'black monk', they all observed a variant of the sixth-century Rule of St Benedict, although not organized as yet into an Order. No comparable houses had survived the Viking settlement of Yorkshire. And it was the desolation of the Christian North, leaving today only the slightest of memorials – a crypt at Ripon, some churchyard crosses, foundations under the turf at Whitby – which inspired a new post-Conquest missionary endeavour.

The initiative, despite the times, was almost entirely Anglo-Saxon. Its purpose was less conversion than the rescue and rehabilitation of Northumbria's plundered saints and of the houses where their relics had been honoured. Three companions, only one of them a Norman, set out from Evesham Abbey (Worcestershire) in 1073–4. Taking their tone from Bede, what they conveyed to the North was a profound respect for its monastic past which most Normans would have found impossible to share.

Their success was almost embarrassingly complete. Shortly after their arrival, as had been their purpose, monastic life was re-established at Jarrow, Bede's old home. Next to be resettled, as would-be monks jostled to join them, were Monkwearmouth (1075) and Whitby (1077), with another party splitting off for St Mary's Abbey, York, halting briefly at Lastingham (1087) on the way. Of most significance in the long term was the rehabilitation of St Cuthbert, entrusted to monks from Jarrow and Monkwearmouth when Durham Cathedral, in 1083, was given over by its Norman bishop to their care. It was Cuthbert, above all, who became the North's patron saint, while the prior of Durham, custodian of Cuthbert's shrine, rose quickly to pre-eminence among landowners of the region: a great magnate as much as a priest.

Durham's estates stretched north into Scotland and south into Yorkshire. Yet the attraction of Yorkshire for French-speaking Benedictines remained restricted, not least by the shadow of St

▲ Benedict of Monte Cassino (*c.* 480– *c.* 550) was the founding father of western monasticism. He was the author of a firm but workable Rule, still widely used as a manual for the monastic life, and frequently reverted to by reformers. (British Library)

◀ To distinguish them from the Cistercians, known as 'white monks' from the colour of their robes, the Benedictines came to be called 'black monks', a description much less flattering to their calling. Here, a monk of the rich Benedictine community at York Abbey (St Mary's) makes his profession to his abbot (*left*). (Bodleian Library)

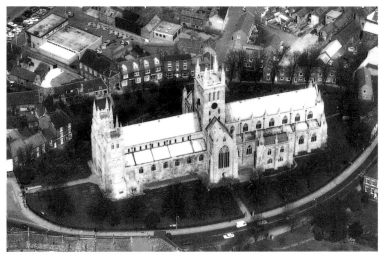

◀ Selby was one of only three great 'black monk' houses in Yorkshire. Its huge church, further extended (like Whitby) in the thirteenth and fourteenth centuries, was preserved for parish use at the Suppression of 1539. Featuring work of all periods, it starts with a Norman crossing and with the exceptionally grand triple-tier arcades of a cathedral-like nave which took much of the twelfth century to complete. (Cambridge)

Cuthbert. In the event, one other major 'black monk' abbey at Selby, with Whitby and York, exhausted Benedictine enterprise in the county. Furthermore, those abbeys in Normandy which had profited so greatly in English estates following the Conquest, never won more than a toehold in the North-East. Among them, Marmoutier successfully established a dependent priory at Holy Trinity, York, with attached cells at Headley and at Allerton Mauleverer. The monks of Aumale and of St Wandrille maintained outposts, later described as 'alien' priories, at Burstall and at Ecclesfield respectively. But that was virtually the sum total of their achievement. Even the highly regarded Cluniacs, most prestigious of the monastic 'families' of the day, made little real headway in the county. Pontefract Priory, founded in the 1090s, was their only permanent establishment before its own offshoot, the much later Monk Bretton (1153–5). Pontefract hid below the bulk of a huge baronial stronghold, family headquarters of Robert de Lacy.

▼ Cluniacs from Pontefract settled Monk Bretton (pictured here) in the 1150s. But disputes between the two houses eventually led to a separation of Monk Bretton from the Cluniac 'family', after which the priory made common cause with the Benedictines. Cluny and her many daughter houses had flourished especially during the second half of the eleventh century, under the direction of the great Abbot Hugh (1049–1109). However, by the mid-twelfth century the movement had lost general favour. It found patronage only amongst those who, as at Pontefract and Monk Bretton, were already committed to its support. Adam Fitzswane, founder of Monk Bretton, was the son of a major Pontefract benefactor. Monk Bretton itself was never rich. (Tony Marshall)

The Regular Canons

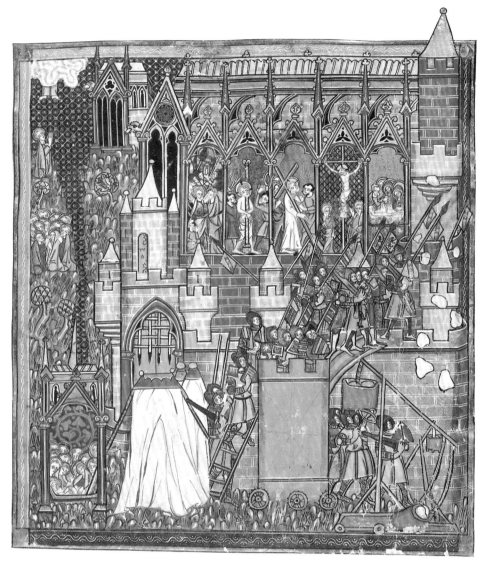

◀ When Pope Urban II preached the First Crusade at Clermont in November 1095, few would have placed their bets on its success. At that time, it was not even clear that the objective of the Crusaders was Jerusalem. All the more remarkable, therefore, was the fall of that city (shown here under siege) less than four years later, shortly followed by the foundation of the Latin Kingdom of Jerusalem and by a prolonged, if precarious, Christian presence in the Holy Land. A miracle had been vouchsafed by God. Reassured of His existence, the devout pressed forward with pious works, including the support of the regular canons. (Bibliothèque Nationale, Paris)

▲ Augustinian canons, who undertook many of the more burdensome tasks in the medieval church including the care of parish churches, were usually too busy to be saints. An exception was St John of Bridlington (pictured here in the black habit of his order), prior of that important Yorkshire house between 1362 and his death in 1379. Prior John was both a practical administrator and a model of devotion. He was one of two Yorkshire saints — St John of Beverley (*d.* 721) was the other — invoked by Henry V at Agincourt in 1415, when they put to flight the holy armoury of the French. (British Library)

B enedictine weakness in the county is one explanation of the generosity of Yorkshire's welcome to later monks. Another is the pressure of world events. Within a decade of the foundation of Pontefract Priory, Christian knights had broken through to Jerusalem. Challenged by the miracle of the First Crusade, few could now question the existence of God or the authority of His chosen mouthpiece, the Pope.

In Yorkshire, several consequences followed. Most direct was the arrival of the military orders – the Hospitallers and especially the Templars – as landowners in the county from the 1140s. They were to use their wealth to support the continuing struggle with Muslim forces in the Holy Land. However, of more importance overall were new perceptions in the faith, as hostile to the lay proprietor as to the pagan. For too long, God's possessions had been treated as though they were private property. Even before the First Crusade, the campaign against lay intervention in church affairs had been gathering force. After it, there was no stopping the reformers.

Attention quickly turned to the ownership of parish churches, many of which had originated as the estate chapels of lay landowners, whose heirs saw them still as a source of revenue. But this, in the new

▲ Bolton Priory, unlike the urban Bridlington, is beautifully set in rural isolation: as remote as a house of Cistercians. In common with other Augustinian houses, Bolton lived off its parish churches. It was successful also as an agricultural estate, especially under the entrepreneurial John of Laund (*c.* 1285–1331). Prior John was a great farmer. But he lived to see his community's temporary bankruptcy and dispersal in 1320, following the harvest failures and Scottish raids of the preceding decade. Another notable prior was Richard Mone, who began Bolton's west tower in 1520. No more lucky than Prior John in the final event, Richard had his work cut short at the Dissolution.

religious climate, was becoming less acceptable. And from the mid-1090s, if not before, the pressure was on to find appropriate homes for the churches and tithes which, as one landowner put it, 'I could not myself keep in my own hand or have at my disposal'. None were better equipped to assume these responsibilities than the newly forming communities of Augustinian canons – priests who had found shelter under the Rule of St Augustine, that 'kind master' who 'drew his brethren to live together and tempered the rigour of his rule to their infirmity'. Fortuitously, the canons' arrival in England coincided with the start of a new and vigorous reign, attracting the patronage of Henry I (1100–35) and his court.

Utility and fashion thus combined in Yorkshire, from the early twelfth century, to open the county to the regular canons, equipped (as monks were not) to undertake the cure of souls in the parishes. There was land to spare, and Yorkshire's Augustinian houses came to rank among the wealthiest of that Order. Of these, Bridlington and Bolton, Gisborough and Kirkham, founded within a decade of each other between 1113 and 1122, have all left impressive remains. Such communities appealed to practical men who, in giving away as patrons something they would have had to give anyway, won permanent recognition in the process. Parish churches, important in the endowment of each of these new houses, accounted for a large part of the canons' revenues. They were to keep those churches in reasonable order, and to pray for their founders in perpetuity.

▲ The parish church (*top*) at Gisborough, served by the canons, was sited immediately north of their priory church and literally under its shadow. This relationship was often repeated. It occurs again in Yorkshire, for example, at Premonstratensian Easby, where the parish church and the canons' refectory almost touch. The arrangement suited both parties. Shared churches were the cause of much dispute. It was frequently better, the canons found, to build their parishioners a church of their own. (Airviews, Manchester)

◄ Bridlington Priory, now in Humberside, was one of the wealthiest of the English Augustinian houses. Its nave is an ambitious thirteenth-century rebuilding, of high cost and majestic scale. At the Dissolution, only the nave (in use by the parish) was preserved. The only other relic of Bridlington Priory today is its gatehouse.

The White Monks

The Augustinians met a practical need. They were the 'Marthas' of Holy Church, labouring in the parishes. They ran almshouses, hospitals and schools. But their contribution to the life of the spirit was less apparent. It was the Cistercians – the 'Marys' – who mined that rich vein, and who carried off huge rewards as a consequence.

Yorkshire, still comparatively barren of monks, became the prime target of Bernard of Clairvaux, charismatic leader of the Cistercians. Bernard spoke to princes as an equal. 'In your land', he told Henry I in 1131, 'there is a possession of my Lord and your Lord . . . I have arranged for it to be taken back, and have sent men from our army who will (if it is not displeasing to you) seek it out, recover it and restore it with a firm hand.' 'And this', wrote a later chronicler, 'is what was done. His men were received with honour by the king and the kingdom, and they established new fortifications in the province of York. They constructed the abbey which is called Rievaulx, which was the first plantation of the Cistercian Order in the province of Yorkshire. Those who were sent were holy men, being monks who glorified God in the practice of poverty. They dwelt in peace with all men, although they warred with their own bodies and with the old enemy. They

▲ Cistercians believed in the virtue of manual labour, with which they filled what remained of a busy day between prayer and spiritual reading. What the monks could not do, they entrusted to lay brethren: illiterate 'draught oxen of Christ', often highly skilled, who were also part of their community. Lay brethren were masons and carpenters, ploughmen, dairymen and shepherds. They took charge of the 'granges' (the abbey's outlying estates), but also cared for the home farm and the business of the great court, being housed for that purpose in the west claustral range, where they had their own dormitory and refectory. (Bibliothèque Municipale, Dijon)

◀ The west range at Fountains, stretching south from the abbey church, is a fine example of the high quality accommodation which the Cistercians provided for their lay brethren. In this large and wealthy community, a long dormitory (now roofless) extends over a finely vaulted undercroft (still intact), part of which was used as the brothers' refectory, the rest as offices and stores.

showed forth the discipline of Clairvaux whence they came, and by works of piety they spread the sweet savour of their mother-abbey, as it were, a strong perfume from their own house. The story spread everywhere that men of outstanding holiness and perfect religion had come from a far land; that they had converse with angels in their dwelling; and that by their virtues they had glorified the monastic name. Many therefore were moved to emulate them by joining this company whose hearts had been touched by God. Thus very soon they grew into a great company. . .'.

In Yorkshire alone, that great company came to include no fewer

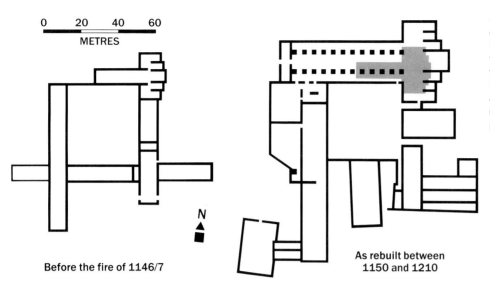

0 20 40 60
METRES

N

Before the fire of 1146/7

As rebuilt between
1150 and 1210

◀ Such was the appeal of Fountains, found-ed in 1132, that its first church was almost immediately too small. Here the plans of the first and second monasteries are con-trasted. The increase in scale is particu-larly evident in the church itself, although obvious also round the cloister. (After G. Coppack, *Archaeologia* 108 [1986], p. 182)

than eight major houses: Rievaulx and Fountains, Byland, Jervaulx and Meaux, Roche, Kirkstall and Salley (now in Lancashire). Only Meaux, of the eight, has left few remains, the others displaying a degree of investment which would be difficult to parallel elsewhere. In the deep winter of 1132, the first settlers at Fountains – dissident Benedictines from York Abbey – had taken shelter under rocks in a narrow valley 'uninhabited for all the centuries back, thick set with thorns, and fit rather to be the lair of wild beasts than the home of human beings'. Yet this 'place of horror and vast solitude' was transformed within the decade into a demi-paradise, attracting such numbers as to require rebuilding on more than twice the scale originally projected. To Rievaulx also, under its saintly Abbot Ailred, there flowed 'from foreign nations and distant lands a stream of monks who needed brotherly mercy and true compassion, and there they found the peace and sanctity without which no man can see God'.

Recruitment at this level – there is said to have been a community of six hundred monks, lay brethren and servants at Rievaulx before Ailred's death in 1167 – was the direct consequence of the Cistercians' reputation. At Rievaulx certainly, although not at all houses, even the poor and the simple were made welcome. Thus Rievaulx's immediate 'family' grew swiftly to include Warden (Bedfordshire), Revesby (Lincolnshire) and Rufford (Nottinghamshire), together with two of the wealthiest Scottish houses at David I's Melrose and Dundrennan. Fountains gave birth to Newminster and Kirkstead, Louth Park and Woburn, Kirkstall, Vaudey and Meaux, all within the space of two decades. Nor were Cistercians the only monks to benefit from the

▲ St Bernard, speaking here in his chapter-house at Clairvaux, was an orator of extra-ordinary power. Mothers, it was said, locked their sons away on his approach. Yet despite such precautions, recruitment flourished and Bernard's 'army' continued to grow. Before Bernard's death in 1153, his white-clad Cistercians had found a wel-come throughout the West, with some five hundred houses already founded. (Musée Condé, Chantilly)

◀ The plan of Roche Abbey is seen excep-tionally complete from the air. Only the east end of the church is upstanding. South of the church, in its usual position, is the clear space of the cloister (*centre*), with the lay brothers' west range to the left and the monks' quarters (including their projecting chapter-house) to the right. Between these is the north–south rectangle of the former refectory, cut by the dark channel of Roche's main drain, economically placed to carry away the waste of both kitchen and rere-dorters (the latrines at the end of each dormitory).

▲ Rievaulx Abbey, settled by Bernard's own men, was the first of eight major Cistercian houses in twelfth-century Yorkshire. Under Abbot Ailred (1147–67) especially, Rievaulx's company grew so large that the church 'was crowded with the brethren like bees in a hive'. In contrast to this activity, the abbey's site was wild and lonely, as was to be the case in most Cistercian houses, deliberately secluded from the world.

◄ The parish church of Old Malton is a battered fragment of a once important Gilbertine priory. It lacks aisles, choir, and much of the former nave. Only one of its western towers has been preserved. Yet this was among the greater of St Gilbert's single-sex priories, intended for canons alone. It had extensive estates in eastern Yorkshire, including granges run on the Cistercian model which Gilbert — the founder of England's only native monastic order — sensibly took as his guide.

fashion they promoted. Their Savigniac competitors, favoured by King Stephen, merged with the Cistercians in 1147. Two Yorkshire houses, Byland and Jervaulx, came from that Savigniac stable. Cistercians inspired the Gilbertines, England's only native order; they furnished a model for the Premonstratensians and an example to the nuns, similarly entering their period of expansion. Early in the 1150s, Yorkshire had Gilbertines in residence at Watton and Malton; there were Premonstratensians at Easby, near Richmond Castle. Both orders went on to establish other Yorkshire houses, although never in such numbers as the nuns.

▼ Easby Abbey was a community of Premonstratensian 'white' canons. It was among the first houses of that order to be established in England, founded in 1155. Like the Cistercians, on whom they modelled themselves in many ways, the Premonstratensians favoured remote riverine settings. They were not generally a wealthy order, and Easby's buildings are far from lavish. Nevertheless, an episode of prosperity in about 1300 enabled the canons to rebuild their refectory (*centre*) in fine style. Their west range (*left*) had been remodelled rather earlier, to accommodate both their dormitory and a guesthouse.

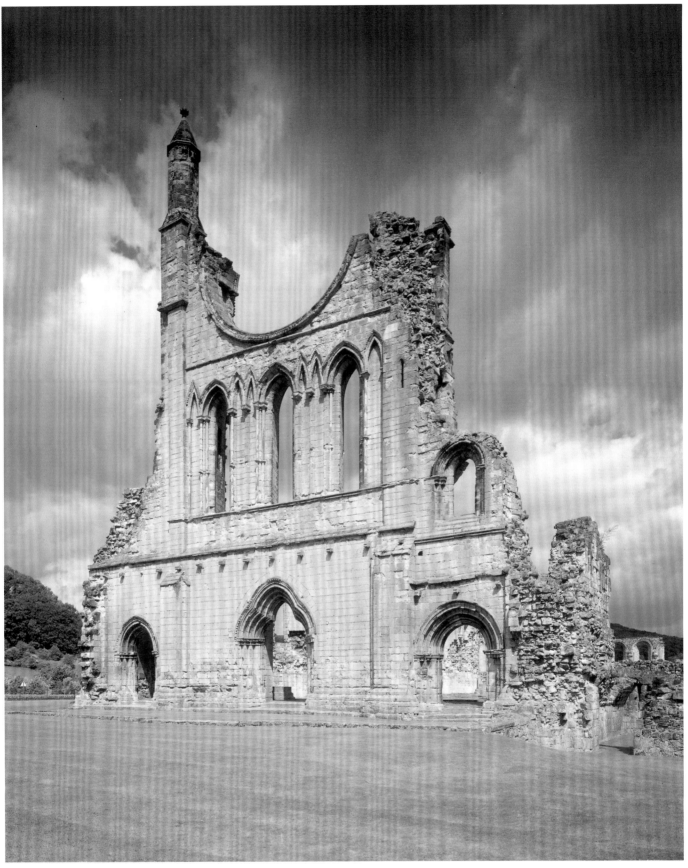

▲ Byland's west front is one of the triumphs of English Transitional, midway between Romanesque (round arches) and Gothic (pointed). A great rose window, of which only the bottom arc is preserved, crowned this ornate facade. Such architectural flamboyance would never have been tolerated in a Cistercian church of the first generation. At Byland, it may be accounted for partly by date (1200–25), and partly also by Savigniac origins: a congregation less severe than the Cistercian.

13

The Nuns

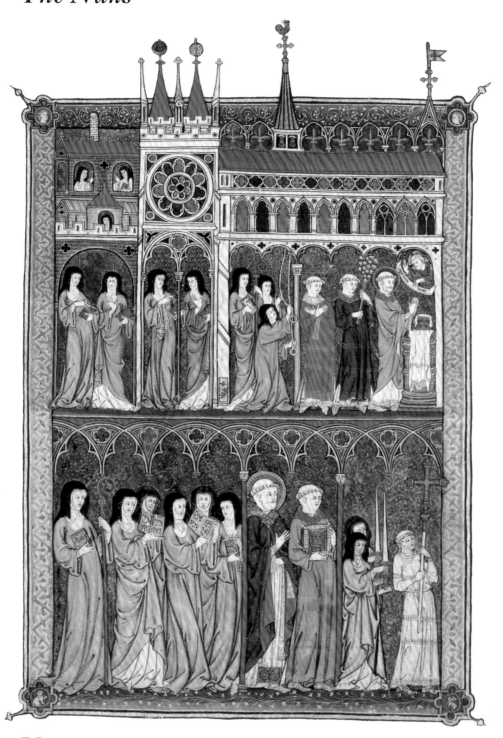

Yorkshire's nunneries, in the days of St Hilda, had included houses of singular distinction. Whitby Abbey, in particular, had set a standard of excellence from Hilda's coming there in 657, its nuns learning 'to observe strictly the virtues of justice, devotion and chastity and other virtues too, but above all things to continue in peace and charity . . . no one was rich, no one was in need, for they had all things in common and none had any private property.' Yet nothing of this pious and well regulated routine had survived the Viking onslaught of 867 or the long, barren years that ensued. Yorkshire was as empty of nunneries in 1066 as it was of communities of monks.

It was the new monasticism of St Bernard and his contemporaries which brought the nuns back into the county. Nuns had played no part in the post-Conquest Mission to the North. But the preaching of the hermit monks – of St Bernard himself and of St Norbert of Xanten,

▲ Nuns had played an important role in the first Christian settlement of Northumbria. They returned to Yorkshire again in the mid-twelfth century, but never recovered their earlier prominence. Here, in a French miniature of about 1300, nuns are shown at prayer. They are led by their priests, usually regular canons, being unable to celebrate mass on their own. (British Library)

14

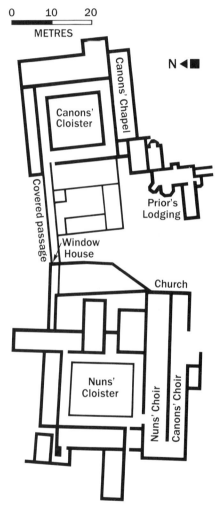

◀ The parish church at Nun Monkton is one of the few major relics of a Yorkshire nunnery. Seen here from the west, it is a building of high quality, with fine lancet windows in the Early English style, attributable to *c.* 1240. Yet below these are features – a formal west portal and double flanking niches – some sixty years earlier in date. The quality of the masonry changes also, and what seems to have happened is that the whole lower part of the nave was completed first, before funds were raised by a later generation to proceed to the next phase of the building programme. Nun Monkton was not a wealthy community. It had to seize its chances when it could.

▲ Gilbert of Sempringham was almost alone in his period in fully meeting the aspirations of English nuns. His order began as a double congregation of nuns and canons, and Watton Priory, founded in *c.* 1150, became the wealthiest double house of the Gilbertines. Watton's plan was recovered in excavations at the beginning of this century. It shows the canons' cloister separated from the nuns' by a wall, in which a 'window house' provided the only (carefully supervised) break. Both nuns and canons shared the same church, but were divided even so by a spine wall.(After St John Hope, *Arch. J.* 58 [1901])

originator of the Premonstratensians – made converts of women as well as men. And it was certainly no accident that Archbishop Thurstan of York, patron of the Cistercians at Fountains, should also have been the founder of Yorkshire's first post-Conquest nunnery, at Clementhorpe within a mile of his cathedral. Thurstan's initiative, datable to between 1125 and 1133, was not immediately followed by a rush of similar foundations. However, the pace had quickened markedly before the mid-century. The county's eventual total of twenty-four nunneries, fully half of which claimed association with the Cistercians, was never exceeded elsewhere.

One other Yorkshire house, the Gilbertine priory at Watton in the East Riding, provided for a double community of nuns and canons, separated only by a wall. There was nothing necessarily scandalous about arrangements of this kind. They had a long and venerable history in the North. But St Bernard's personal friendship with the Englishman, St Gilbert, did not extend to his women. Largely on their account, a proposed merger between the two Orders was rejected. Ever afterwards, the Cistercians stayed wary of their nuns, as much on grounds of finance as of discipline.

What they dreaded was the poverty of the nunneries. With the exception of the Gilbertine Watton, all the Yorkshire nunneries were small, weak and poor. Lacking the accumulated wealth of the ancient royal nunneries of Wessex, they had commonly been founded by landowners of only middling rank, seeking to make provision for pious relatives. One of the earlier of these foundations was the Benedictine Nun Monkton, established for their daughter Maud, its first prioress, by William and Juetta de Arches. Nun Monkton is exceptional among the Yorkshire nunneries for the scale and the quality of its remains, only Swine having anything to parallel it. But although better off by far than the majority of its Yorkshire sisters, Nun Monkton was never a community of great wealth. With an income at suppression in 1536 of only £72, it had just a fifth of the resources of St Gilbert's double priory at Watton. When the Cistercian monks of Fountains disbanded three years later, they had revenues fully fifteen times as large.

Discipline

The common ground of twelfth-century monasticism, taken again by the Mendicant Friars in the following century, was a return to the simplicity of the Apostolic Life. Hermit monks saw themselves, without pretence, as 'the poor men of Christ'. As Stephen of Muret had once put it to his Grandmontines: 'My brethren, you will go to some poor place where there are neither buildings nor books, and you will not shrink from poverty. A wood is a suitable spot in which to build a cell and live by toil . . . I have remained in my hermitage for nearly fifty years, some of them years of plenty, others of scarcity, but I have always had enough. So will it be with you . . .'. And so indeed it was with the Grandmontines of Yorkshire, settled at Grosmont (near Whitby) in 1204, to survive there in Egton Forest until 1536 on an annual income of only £12.

Nothing remains of Grosmont, nor do the Yorkshire abbeys, where they have survived, add greatly to the record of such austerities. Yet contemporaries had once seen them very differently. One of these was William of Malmesbury, no Cistercian himself, who started an account of the early years of the Order by recording its repute as 'the surest road to heaven'. Burgundian Cîteaux, 'a place formerly densely covered with woods but now so translucent from the abundant piety of its monks that it is not undeservedly esteemed to know God himself', had built its quality on the sternest of disciplines. 'Certainly,' continued William, 'many of their regulations seem severe, and more particularly these: they wear nothing made with furs or linen . . . They have two tunics with cowls, but no additional garment in winter . . . They sleep clad and girded, and never after matins return to their beds . . . so intent are they on their Rule that they think no jot nor tittle of it should be disregarded . . . No one is ever absent from the daily offices nor from compline, except the sick . . . The abbot allows himself no indulgence beyond the others, and is everywhere present, everywhere attending his flock . . . They never leave the cloister but for the purpose of labour, nor do they ever speak, either there or elsewhere,

▲ The Cistercians, at their best, were 'a model for all monks, a mirror for the diligent, a spur to the indolent'. They prided themselves, among other things, on simplicity in dress, wearing garments of rough un-dyed cloth which caused them to be described as 'white monks'. (Bibliothèque Municipale, Dijon)

◄ The unadorned drum columns of the nave arcades at Fountains are typical of Cistercian architecture of the first period. Bernard loved Fountains and Henry Murdac, its third abbot (1143–53), under whom the community's huge expansion took place. Like his patron St Bernard, Murdac was harshly antagonistic to over-ornament in architecture, which he saw as a distraction from worship.

◀ Little remains of Rievaulx's nave. Nevertheless, its unornamented column bases (*left foreground*) are precious evidence of the austerity of an order which began as disciplined in its architecture as in its dress.

save only to the abbot or prior. They continue unwearied in the canonical hours . . . While they bestow care on the stranger and the sick, they inflict intolerable mortifications on their own bodies for the salvation of their souls . . . to sum up all the things which are or can be said of them, the Cistercians at the present day are a model for all monks, a mirror for the diligent, a spur to the indolent.'

The model could not last, and Cistercian life and buildings, from the third quarter of the twelfth century, had ceased to set a standard of austerity. But there are indications still, at two Yorkshire abbeys, of this early simplicity of life-style. The churches at Rievaulx and at Fountains were huge in scale, with nothing economical about their layout. Yet the piers of their naves were utterly plain and unadorned.

▼ The chancel at Rievaulx, of which this is the south arcade, is a lavish rebuilding of about 1200. It has none of the simplicity of the earlier Cistercian architecture on the same site, being remote from the precepts of St Bernard of Clairvaux, whose monks had first come there in 1132.

◀ St Benedict had said: 'As often as any important business has to be done in the monastery, let the abbot call together the whole community and himself set forth the matter.' In practice, monks met daily in their chapter-house for debate and spiritual correction. As here at Jervaulx, the chapter-house was accorded a place of special prominence, usually at the centre of the east claustral range.

Contrast what is left of Rievaulx's severe nave with the triple-tiered arcades of its later choir and presbytery, extended from just two bays to seven. Then compare the vast simplicity of Fountains' drum-like piers with the complex blind arcading and soaring multiple shafts of the early thirteenth-century Chapel of the Nine Altars. The extensions in each case are of a more relaxed generation. They belong to a period of secure prosperity, when the fine edge of ardour had been dulled.

That early primitive ardour, unselfconsciously displayed, is nowhere better evidenced than in a near-contemporary story about St Gilbert. This 'clearly extraordinary man . . . of singular grace in the care of women' had grown old and 'most unsuited for the purposes of lust' when a nun of his community revealed her love for him. Gilbert's horror was genuine, and his remedy nothing less than heroic. The next day, after preaching chastity to his nuns, Gilbert shed all his clothes and paraded naked before them, 'hairy, emaciated, scabrous and wild'. Pointing to a crucifix: 'Behold', he said, 'the man who should be duly desired by a woman consecrated to God and a bride of Christ.' Then, indicating himself: 'Behold the body on account of which a miserable woman has made her body and soul worthy of being lost in Hell.'

▲ Ailred, abbot of Rievaulx (1147–67), joined the community in 1134 as one of its first English recruits. In 1143, he left briefly to take charge of Revesby, but returned to Rievaulx in 1147, remaining there as abbot till he died. Ailred kept an open door at Rievaulx. During his time, wrote Ailred's friend and biographer Walter Daniel, 'those who were restless in the world and to whom no religious house gave entry, coming to Rievaulx the mother of mercy and finding the gates wide open, freely entered therein.' After his death, Ailred's relics were the focus of a cult. (Bibliothèque Municipale, Douai)

▲ Fantasies fed, then as now, on the alleged misbehaviour of nuns: in this fourteenth-century Flemish illumination, a naked man wheels nuns home, following a night of dissipation. The punishment for actual misdemeanours could be horrific, as is evident from a story recorded by Ailred of Rievaulx concerning the Gilbertine Watton Priory. At Watton, we are told, a young nun and a canon became lovers. 'O close your eyes' wrote Ailred, 'cover your ears. She went out a virgin of Christ, and she soon returned an adulteress.' The punishment, on discovery, was terrible. Beaten, imprisoned, chained and starved, the pregnant nun was released only to be required to castrate her lover, after which a zealous sister, overcome by rage, took hold of the severed parts and crammed them into the girl's mouth. 'I praise not the deed but the zeal', remarked Ailred, 'and I approve not the shedding of blood but so great a striving of the nuns against evil. What would they not suffer, what would they not do to preserve chastity, those who could do such things to avenge it?'

▲ The Chapel of the Nine Altars at Fountains, like Rievaulx's surviving chancel, is a later rebuilding of the east end of the abbey church. Both suggest more spacious days and a more relaxed regime as each community came to terms with its wealth.

BYLAND ABBEY: *Life in a Cistercian monastery*

▼ The day began early at Byland Abbey, one of Yorkshire's big Cistercian communities. The monks left their *dormitory* (1) shortly after two in the morning for Matins in the *choir* (2) of the abbey church. Rising again for Lauds at five, they remained at prayer until dawn (Prime), then returning to their devotions at regular intervals until sunset (Compline) sent them back to their beds.

Everything in the layout of a monastic house supported this unvarying routine. The monks exercised in the garden of Byland's big central *cloister* (3), and read devotional works in the shelter of its alleys. They ate in silence in the *refectory* (4), met for correction and debate in the *chapter-house* (5), gossiped in the *warming-house* (6), and retreated to the *infirmary* (7) when sick.

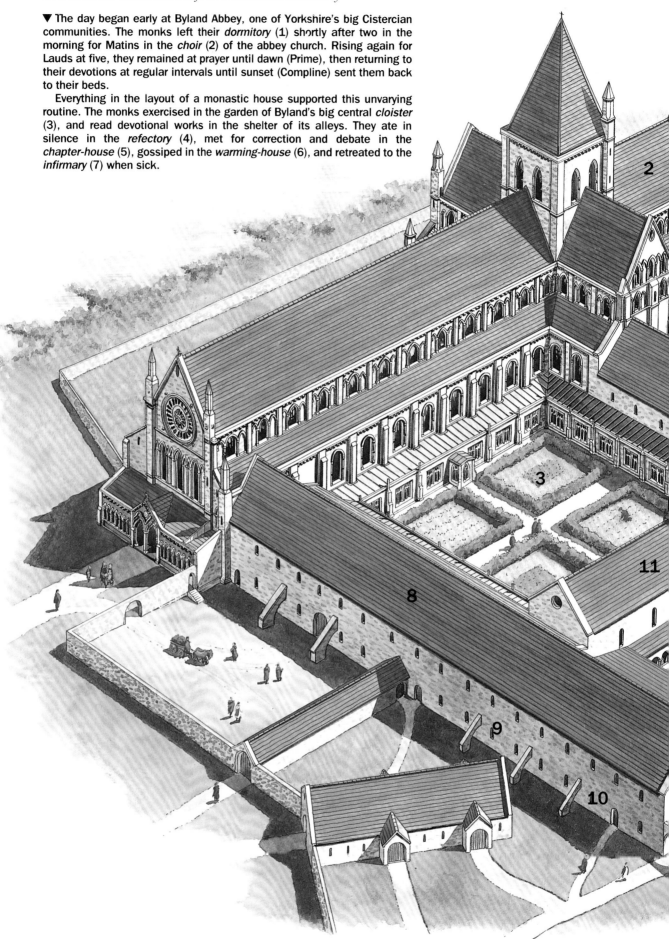

All the daily tasks of farm and garden were entrusted at Byland to illiterate lay brethren. It was for these that the long west range was provided, with separate *dormitory* (8) on the first floor, and *refectory* (9) and *infirmary* (10) below. Only the great *kitchen* (11) was shared with the monks. Such distinctions came to be seen as invidious. Lay brethren rebelled or ceased to come forward. Recruitment slowed and then stopped altogether.

Meanwhile, the monks themselves had relaxed their regime. The fifteenth-century *meat kitchen* (12) at Byland is a characteristic addition of the last period of English monasticism. There, dietary regulations were effectively ignored, and Byland's monks, in the comfort of an adjoining heated *misericord* (13), ate meat at all times except Lent. Proudest of these 'proud epicures' was the abbot of Byland, increasingly remote from his community. The abbot lived in his own *lodgings* (14), to the east of the monks' dormitory, linked to it by a first-floor *rere-dorter*, or common lavatory (15). A separate *pentice* (16) sheltered the abbot's progress to the hugely ornate choir where he presided in great dignity as superior.

(Simon Hayfield)

The Friars

Before the friars first came to Yorkshire in the late 1220s, the expansion of the older orders (the so-called 'possessioners') was at an end. After Meaux in 1151, there were no new Cistercian foundations in the county. The last Gilbertine house was the hospital at Ellerton, founded in or before 1209. The Premonstratensians had halted on the upland pastures of Egglestone (1198), always among the smallest and poorest houses of their Order. Even the more adaptable Augustinians managed only one new foundation after 1218, and that was at Haltemprice a century later, when the canons came again into temporary prominence as the custodians of chantry chapels for the dead.

The friars multiplied quickly. There were Dominicans at York from 1227, Franciscans from 1230 and Carmelites from 1253, each colonising further houses from that base. Austin friars had set up at Tickhill in 1260, to reach York some twelve years later. In an expansion which continued well into the next century, and which was frequently resisted by other clerics, almost every Yorkshire town attracted one or more of the four principal fraternities of Mendicants. Yet only indirectly were the friars a threat to existing houses of monks. Few friaries ever accumulated landed property of any substance. The brothers maintained themselves by begging. They preached to a new urban audience, and found a fresh source of patronage in the burgesses. What they snatched was the bread of the parish priest.

Rivalries in the parishes, whether for congregations or dues, must be one explanation why so few friary churches survived the suppressions of 1538–9. In Yorkshire, certainly, the solitary tower of the Franciscans of Richmond stands almost alone to recall them. Yet the friars had

▲ Friars were known especially for their preaching, through which (in the view of their clerical detractors) they stole the hearts and entered the pockets of their listeners. In this carving, from a Beverley Minster misericord, a fox (in the habit of a friar) is seen preaching to geese. The Minster was an ancient collegiate foundation, wealthy and resistant to change. Dominicans and Franciscans, both resident in the town from the mid-thirteenth century, preached a life of abstinence and of evangelical poverty, highly offensive to the wealthy rectors-choral.

◀ Few friary buildings survive in England. Almost always in towns, they were vulnerable to re-development for many purposes. One of the few is the handsome tower of the Franciscans of Richmond. It once separated the friars' choir from their preaching nave, in which they offered instruction to the townspeople. Richly finished with pinnacles and pierced parapets, the tower is a memorial to late-medieval burgess piety, which resulted in a harvest of legacies to the friars denied to most monks of the same period.

▲ Egglestone Abbey, poor and remote, was the last Premonstratensian settlement in Yorkshire (now in Co. Durham). Fashions in religion were changing fast. From 1227, when the Dominicans came to York, donors favoured the friars. Choir monks and canons, whatever their order, had to subsist as best they might on their capital.

moved mountains in their day. While monks and canons locked themselves away, increasingly out of sympathy with their folk, the friars took Christ to the market-place. They preached with more resonance than the parish priests, understood doctrine better, confessed the living with greater expertise, and buried the dead with more compassion.

Only two other religious communities, both of them Carthusian, similarly kept their hold on Yorkshire sentiment. Kingston upon Hull (from 1377) and Mount Grace (from 1398) promised that sublimation of the spirit – most regarded for being hardest won – of the silent and unworldly recluse. They were all that the Mendicants could not be: their exact yet necessary opposites.

▶ In this Yorkshire manuscript sketch, a Carthusian is seen reading outside his cell. Just such a cell has been reconstructed in the north claustral range at Mount Grace, and several others are clearly visible in plan. They were spacious enough but were cold and austere, and could never have been anything different. One early Carthusian, Alexander of Lewes, had found the Order's regime altogether too much for him. Writing of Witham, in late twelfth-century Somerset, he complained: 'The whole land is full of communities of monks, and the mutual support provided by the communal life supplies us with a sufficiently good example of religious perfection. Here, alone and without companionship, we become torpid and dull through boredom, seeing no one for days at a time whose example can inspire us, and having only the walls which shut us in to look at.' Alexander was a Cluniac: a migrant searcher after truth. 'Since we know better,' he argued, 'we must not and cannot endure this unprofitable and narrow way of life any longer. We are going to seek something saner.' (British Library)

▲ A conjectural reconstruction of Mount Grace as it may have looked in the fifteenth century. The cloister (*left*) is seen from the west. Round it are the monks' two-storeyed cells, each with its own little garden. Carthusians received their food through hatches from the cloister. Once in their cells, they had all they needed, listed in the customal of the Order: two spoons, two pots, a jug, a bread knife, a salt cellar, etc, with clothing (two hair-shirts and four pairs of socks) and with a straw pallet, under coarse woollen coverlets, as bed. (Alan Sorrell)

▲ Mount Grace Priory is unique in England as a relic of the Carthusian regime. Other monks lived in common. The Carthusians, in contrast, rarely met their brethren, passing the long day in the isolation of their cells from which, only occasionally, they surfaced. In this air view of Mount Grace, the great cloister is seen in the top centre, with the church just below it, to the south. Carthusian churches were always small, being relatively little used by the community. They were closed to outsiders and had, as here (*left of the tower*), only the most stunted of naves. South and west of the church were additional courts (*bottom centre*), accommodating the guesthouse — today's mansion — and farm buildings. (Airviews, Manchester)

25

The Monk-Builders

The monk's lot is harsh. He cannot hope to see his face in his son's. Lacking the memorials of other men, he may seek to find a substitute in building. Many monastic communities, over a century and more, dwelt continuously in the turmoil of a building site. At some, the work of new construction never ceased.

What gave special drive to contemporary building programmes was the widely shared prosperity of monastic landowners. Raul Glaber, a Cluniac monk of the early eleventh century, saw this launched in the millennial year AD1000. 'It was as if', he wrote, 'the whole earth, having cast off the old by shaking itself, were clothing itself everywhere in the white robe of the Church.' And for the next three centuries, until towards their end, population was on the increase; rents were rising and wages were falling; the sun smiled reassuringly on record harvests. Particularly fortunate were those Yorkshire abbeys – among them Rievaulx and Byland, Bridlington, Whitby and Gisborough – prominent in the export trade in wool. But monastic agriculture, too, had become more efficient, with home-farming everywhere the norm. Nor could many assets match the all-but-effortless profitability of a popular crowd-pulling relic. No major church of thirteenth-century Yorkshire – from Bolton to Bridlington, Easby to Fountains, Gisborough to Kirkham, Pontefract to Selby, and many more – remained wholly unaffected by the boom.

It was St Hilda's cult, alongside the wool trade, which financed the rebuilding of Whitby Abbey. A huge new choir, begun in the 1220s, set the scale there for all subsequent works. But such ventures might take many decades to complete, even given the co-operation of a saint. Thirty years later, Whitby's crossing had been reached, but its monks were seriously in debt. Work halted, and it was not until long afterwards, well into the next century, that the remodelling of the nave could begin. Midway through a similar programme, the Augustinians of Kirkham found themselves overtaken by events. Early in the thirteenth century, contemporaneously with Whitby, they had embarked on a rebuilding which, had it been completed, must have doubled the size of their priory. They finished a new choir and presbytery, very much larger than the old, but made no more than a beginning on the crossing. They rebuilt their gatehouse with great heraldic display. They re-sited their chapter-house, again much grander than before, yet were never in a position to extend the cloister of which it had been intended as the focus. By the end of the same century, when further construction was abandoned, the canons were £1000 in debt.

At Kirkham, work was never re-started. But priorities anyway were changing. Battered by disasters – by harvest failures and livestock murrains in 1315–22, by Scottish plundering sorties in 1318–19, and by the Black Death of 1348–9 and its successor plagues – Yorkshire's many

▲ Many of Yorkshire's greater monastic houses made their fortunes through sheep-rearing on the Wolds. Yorkshire wool was of superior quality, fetching good prices on the Continent. And it was active participation in this profitable exchange which kept the monks building in the twelfth and thirteenth centuries, when Flemish weavers were especially hungry for English fleece. In this illuminated initial from a St Albans manuscript, a monk is shown shearing one of the sheep to which he owed much of his living. (Bodleian Library, Oxford)

◀ Unlike the friars, who subsisted by begging, the monks were always great agricultural entrepreneurs, frequently among the pioneers of new technology. Here, one of Rievaulx's many windmills is shown on a contemporary relief carving from the abbey. It is a post-mill with heavy sails, placed high on its mound yet easily turned by the miller to face the wind.

▲ At Gisborough Priory, building became a way of life. When the canons decided to rebuild their monastery before the mid-thirteenth century, they hired master masons and settled them and their families in the town. Masons brought up their children at Gisborough; died and were buried in the priory church; left money for the continuation of the works. Then, on 16 May 1289, a terrible fire swept through the church, and building began all over again. Gisborough's surviving east end — its major architectural relic — is of an innovatory Early Decorated design. It is the work of skilled professionals, started (as it were) when the stone was still warm from the blaze. (Thomas Girtin, 1801; Tate Gallery, London)

abbeys took refuge in that sleep from which only the Suppression would awaken them. Benedict's Rule had taken a tumble in the meantime. Every earlier rebuilding had begun with the church or with some other shared facility of the community – with the chapter-house or refectory, warming-house, dormitory or infirmary. In contrast, monastic remodellings of the Later Middle Ages concentrated almost exclusively on private quarters. Nothing was less in harmony with the prescriptions of St Benedict, who had seen private property as 'this most wicked vice', to be 'utterly rooted out of the monastery'.

Most conspicuous of these buildings were the new abbots' lodgings, never grander than at the King's Manor, York. Rebuilt in the 1480s for the abbot of St Mary's, brick was chosen at York as the latest and most fashionable building material, the resulting style being entirely domestic. Similarly comfortable – just like a big private dwelling – was the Prior's Hall at contemporary Watton. Taking their cue from their abbots, others in each community took advantage for themselves of the very general relaxation of the Rule. Refectories were scaled down and meat-kitchens were provided. Cloisters were glazed. Dormitories and infirmaries were partitioned.

That great monk-builder, Abbot Marmaduke Huby of Fountains (1494–1526), won praise in his day as a 'golden and unbreakable column in his zeal for the Order'. Yet Huby presided over a community much relaxed in discipline since first settlement in the 'vast solitude' of

▲ What shows especially clearly in this air view of Kirkham is the huge choir and presbytery (*top right*) with which the canons began, from early in the thirteenth century, an ambitious reconstruction of their church. The work was never finished. They reached the crossing, but failed altogether to rebuild the nave (*top left*), or to complete the proposed expansion of their cloister. (Airviews, Manchester)

▲Kirkham's gatehouse, although badly knocked about, is a building of evident quality. Its tracery and other ornaments are in the Westminster Court Style, the most refined of its time. And it dates to the last quarter of the thirteenth century, when the canons' rebuilding programme, already two generations old, had almost run its course. De Roos patronage had supported that programme. In Kirkham's fine new presbytery, de Roos sepulchres held places of honour, next to the canons' high altar. Here on the gatehouse, de Roos heraldry is prominent again, proclaiming the protection of the lords of Helmsley Castle over the Augustinian custodians of their tombs.

▲ There was seldom a time when builders were entirely absent from a monastery. Here monks of Durham, assisted by an angel, are laying ashlars to speed the good work. The scene is of the late twelfth century. Durham monks were still building in the fifteenth. (British Library)

▲ The east end at Whitby, begun by Abbot Roger in the 1220s, was the first part of the church to be rebuilt. It set the scale for a building programme which lasted over a century, enormously enlarging the abbey church.

29

◀ The important brick mansion of the abbots of York (St Mary's) has been largely hidden under successive remodellings of the sixteenth and seventeenth centuries, including the insertion of this Charles I portal. Yet the huge scale of the abbot's personal lodgings is still obvious. Late in the fifteenth century, when work began on the new lodgings, the abbot's estates had returned to profitability. A prince of the church who was also a great landowner had little choice but to live in fine style.

the Dales. Before him, Abbot Darnton had improved the misericord, where monks both sick and hale could take meat. Fountains' huge thirteenth-century infirmary, inconvenient and draughty, had already been partitioned into separately heated, private chambers. Abbot Huby, for all his zeal, took rule-bending two stages further. Once, Cistercian abbots had denied themselves privilege: Huby rebuilt his personal lodgings in fine style. No tower, originally, had been permitted on Cistercian churches: Huby raised a prodigy as his monument.

Huby's tower at Fountains, of which Furness was the model and Bolton the imitator, shows the spirit of competition still alive in the monasteries, every monk-builder (as he had always done) interpreting God's glory as his own. On the Fountains tower, Marmaduke Huby's initials are accompanied by Latin texts, one of them a special favourite with the abbot: '*Regi autem* . . . Now unto the King eternal, immortal, invisible, the only God, be honour and glory for ever and ever.' Prior Mone of Bolton, who never finished *his* tower, was a little more direct in its dedication: 'In the year of our Lord MVCXX R[ichard Mone] began this foundation, on whose soul God have mercy, Amen.'

▲ Jervaulx's fifteenth-century meat kitchen, of which this was one of the cooking ranges, was a characteristic addition of the Late Middle Ages, when the worst rigours of the Rule were relaxed. Meat, in earlier times, had been permitted only to the sick. By the fifteenth century all Cistercian monks ate meat regularly, usually gathering for that purpose in a heated chamber (the 'misericord'), away from the echoing spaces of an over-large and draughty refectory.

◀ Tower-building was among the vanities discouraged by the earliest Cistercian legislators. The most they would allow was a single-storeyed tower above the crossing. Here at Kirkstall, another lofty, well-windowed storey was added to this base in the sixteenth century. It was put there entirely for effect.

▲ Marmaduke Huby's tower at Fountains Abbey is one of the great prodigy towers of late medieval England. It was quite unnecessary, being hidden away secretively against the cliff-face. Yet it finished off the church as little else could do, and of course might be a place for hanging bells. Abbot Huby's building instinct was aroused. His community was rich, especially so under his guidance. Nothing less would suffice as his cenotaph.

'Bare ruin'd choirs where late the sweet birds sang'

Like the death of an old lady, the suppression of the religious houses, however long anticipated, came suddenly and left a sense of loss. The English abbeys had become, as a Venetian traveller observed, 'enormously rich . . . more like baronial palaces than religious houses'. They were ripe, many believed, for disendowment. But such proposals had been in the air since the mid-fourteenth century. They seemed as far from reality in the early 1530s as when the reformer Wycliffe and his sympathisers had first voiced them.

Martin Luther's Reformation and Henry VIII's break with Rome were the triggers that set off destruction. Certainly, the suppression of the 'little and small abbeys' – resistant to change and guilty (so the Act of 1536 claimed) of 'manifest sin, vicious, carnal, and abominable living' – made reasonable sense. 'Always among good Corn are some Weeds not a few: Yea, very filthy and stinking.' Understandably, houses with fewer than twelve inmates, and with an income of less than £200 a year, were the first to be dissolved by the king's commissioners. But the potential for renewal among the wealthier monasteries was much greater. Just before their closure, while some of the larger communities were truly exhausted and played out, others had re-emerged as centres of learning and discovery, propagators of the Northern Renaissance.

None of this survived beyond 1540. The so-called 'voluntary' surrenders of the greater houses began in 1538. All had gone within a couple of years. Among those shipwrecked and 'dasht all a peeces' was Roche, in southern Yorkshire, a Cistercian house laid waste with exceptional dedication. Michael Sherbrook, native of Rotherham and rector of Wickersley, recalled how, in his youth, he had seen the bells of Roche still in place. Thirty years later, he set down a record of the 'spoil' of the abbey, in progress already on the day the monks left,

▲ Salley (now in Lancashire) was among the 'little and small abbeys' suppressed in 1536. Its community, at twenty-one monks, was at that time larger than most. But it had lost its force of lay brethren long before, showing clearly this deficiency in its plan. In this air view of Salley, the site of the church is towards the bottom of the picture, with a big rectangular choir (*left*) and a spacious crossing and transepts (*centre*). Note, however, the wall which cuts the line of the former nave, just two bays west of the crossing. With no lay brethren to accommodate, Salley's choir-monks maintained only what they needed of their church: in effect, those parts of it – east of the *pulpitum* (screen) – traditionally reserved for themselves. (Crown copyright)

◀ Thomas Cromwell – chancellor, secretary, and vicar-general – was Henry VIII's chief executive in the wholesale suppression of the religious houses. He was a man of great ability, but as brutal and as grasping as this portrait makes him look, feloniously appropriating huge rewards for himself from the pick of the confiscated lands. (National Portrait Gallery)

▲ The monks of Roche were dismissed in 1538, after a pathos-filled site auction of their effects. Their departure was followed by a destruction so complete that, of the church and claustral buildings, only these fragments of the crossing are still upstanding. 'What should I do,' said a participant later: 'might I not as well as others have some Profit of the Spoil of the Abbey? For I did see all would away.' (Tony Marshall)

when 'an Uncle of mine was present, being well acquainted with certain of the Monks there; and when they were put forth of the House, one of the Monks, his Friend, told him that every one of the Convent had given to him his Cell, wherein he lied: wherein was not any thing of Price, but his Bed and Apparell, which was but simple and of small Price. Which Monk willed my Uncle to buy something of him; who said, I see nothing that is worth Money to my use; No said he; give me ii*d* for my Cell Door, which was never made with vs. No said my Uncle, I know not what to do with it (for he was a Young Man unmarried, and then neither stood need of Houses nor Doors). But such Persons as afterward bought their Corn or Hay or such like, found all the doors either open or the Locks and Shackles plucked away, or the Door itself taken away, went in and took what they found, filched it away.'

The policy of Henry VIII's advisers was to destroy the churches first, 'for fear the Birds should build therein again'. And this, Sherbrook tells us, was what happened at Roche, where 'the Church was the first thing that was put to the spoil, and then the Abbat's Lodgine, Dortor, and Frater, with the Cloister and all the Buildings thereabout. . . . It would have pitied any Heart to see what tearing up of the Lead there was, and plucking up of Boards, and throwing down of the Sparres . . . and all things of Price, either spoiled, carped [plucked] away or defaced to the uttermost.'

Strange, Sherbrook thought – and he was not alone – that 'even such Persons were content to spoil them, that seemed not two days before to allow their Religion, and do great Worship and Reverence at their Mattins, Masses and other Service, and all other their doings.' So he embarked on some personal research: 'For the better Proof of this my Saying, I demanded of my Father, thirty years after the Suppression, which had bought part of the Timber of the Church, and all the Timber in the Steeple, with the Bell Frame, with other his Partners therein . . . whether he thought well of the Religious Persons and of the Religion then used? And he told me Yea: For said He, I did see no Cause to the contrary: Well, said I, then how came it to pass you was so ready to destroy and spoil the thing you thought well of? What should I do, said He: might I not as well as others have some Profit of the Spoil of the Abbey? For I did see all would away; and therefore I did as others did.'

▲ Meaux Abbey, a big Cistercian house suppressed in 1539, has left nothing except a tumbled field of earthworks. Yet the plan of Meaux's church (*left*) and of its cloister (*centre*) can still be made out, in this air view of the site, through the rough summertime pasture. (Cambridge)

◀ Nobody was ever better than the Cistercian monk in harnessing water to his ends. At Roche Abbey today, a bright stream still rushes through the conduits of a monastery once dependent on its flow, but abandoned since 1538.

Signposts to the Past

No sooner were the Middle Ages dead and gone, than antiquarians felt the need to resurrect them. Early in the seventeenth century, there were already those enthusiasts, 'strangely thrifty of Time past', who 'goe you forty miles to see a Saints Well, or ruin'd Abbey'. Others, sensitive to decay, began the recording of what was left. 'I thought my self in duty bound', wrote Thomas Southouse about Faversham in 1671, 'to rescue from the teeth of all devouring time and oblivion some memorials concerning the primitive state & condition thereof.' Southouse lived 'within the verge and precincts' of Faversham Abbey, 'expecting it every day to sink under the heavy pressure of its own weight, and lie entombed in the rubbage of its ruins'. Many more, both of his time and later, have continued to draw bitter-sweet satisfaction from the occasional contemplation of 'mournfull ruines'. Blind to the *otiositas* (idleness and tedium) of the monastic life, they recall only its devotion and spacious rituals.

Nowhere are such sensibilities more readily awakened than in Yorkshire. Both Rievaulx and Fountains, originators of the Cistercian presence in the county, were landscaped in the mid-eighteenth century, to become pleasure grounds of the reigning aristocracy. From Duncombe's Rievaulx Terrace, or across the lawns and waters of Aislabie's Studley Royal, the ruins of two huge abbeys confront us

▲ The smooth sward of Rievaulx Terrace stops at a Grecian temple at each end. From this contrived viewpoint, Thomas Duncombe and his guests fed on the melancholy of the Gothic abbey below, deliciously aware of their own sensibility.

▲ Romantics of all periods have been attracted by 'mournfull ruines'. This watercolour of Bolton Priory is by the great landscape-painter Turner (1775–1851). It captures the serenity of a scene which, even now, is as tranquil as when populated by canons. (Trustees of the British Museum)

today, not as they were when the monks yet lived there but as we have since learnt to love them. Jervaulx is now a garden, exceptionally sweet. At Roche, the water still plays as once it foamed through St Bernard's Clairvaux, 'making its way through the many offices of the abbey, it everywhere leaves a blessing behind it'. Bolton and Kirkham, Easby and Egglestone – all have a memorable tranquillity. Mount Grace is for the healing of the spirit. What we cherish, like our predecessors, is their silence.

▲ Jervaulx's ruins are 'Romantick' in decay, now the most lovely of English gardens. Set aside scholarship when you visit this abbey. Its beauty is accessible to us all.

Further Reading

Margaret Aston, 'English ruins and English history: the Dissolution and the sense of the Past', *J. Warburg and Courtauld Inst.*, 36 (1973).

Janet Burton, *The Yorkshire Nunneries in the Twelfth and Thirteenth Centuries*, Borthwick Papers 56, 1979.

Giles Constable, 'Aelred of Rievaulx and the Nun of Watton: an episode in the early history of the Gilbertine Order', *Studies in Church History*, 1978.

David Knowles, *The Monastic Order in England*, Cambridge University Press, 1966 (2nd edition).

David Knowles, *The Religious Orders in England*, 3 volumes, Cambridge University Press, 1979 (paperback).

Colin Platt, *The Abbeys and Priories of Medieval England*, Secker & Warburg, 1984 (paperback).

Michael Sherbrook, 'The Fall of Religious Houses', in *Tudor Treatises* (ed. A. G. Dickens), Yorkshire Archaeological Society Records Series 125, 1959.

Gazetteer and Map

Bolton Priory
At Bolton Abbey, 10km E of Skipton on B6160

Bolton's parish church, in its beautiful riverine setting, was formerly the nave of an Augustinian priory. The canons' roofless choir and transepts also survive, as do the foundations of their claustral ranges to the south. At the west end of the church, the stump of a huge, unfinished tower dates to the early 16c. Note the medieval precinct wall and the great early 14c gatehouse, rebuilt in the 19c as a mansion.

Bridlington Priory
In Bridlington, N of the town centre

The parish church preserves the fine nave, rebuilt at huge expense in the 13c, of one of England's earliest and wealthiest Augustinian priories, founded in *c.* 1115. Everything east of the nave was demolished shortly after the suppression of Bridlington Priory in 1537. A big, late 14c gatehouse is the only survival of the priory's domestic ranges.

Byland Abbey *(English Heritage)*
3km S of A170 between Thirk and Helmsley, near Coxwold village

Byland's Cistercian plan is exceptionally complete and dates to the late 12c. At that time the abbey was built anew on a freshly cleared site and in an ornate, Early Gothic style far removed from the primitive austerities of the Order. Distinctively Cistercian is the full provision for lay brethren in the west range, with a dormitory and refectory of their own. Note also the rare survival here of the lay brothers' 'lane', excluding the brethren from the cloister and keeping the two communities apart.

Easby Abbey *(English Heritage)*
1.5km SE of Richmond on minor road off B6271

Easby was a house of Premonstratensian canons, founded in 1151 and endowed with parish churches, including St Agatha's (next to the canons' refectory) to be visited for its handsome set of 13c wall-paintings. Easby's refectory is a lavish early 14c rebuilding, coinciding in date with an eastward extension of the church and with other evidence of pre-Black Death prosperity in the community. West of the cloister, the dormitory and guest quarters share the same location, where there was drainage into the river below. Because the parish church occupied their usual location, both the infirmary and abbot's lodgings were sited north of the presbytery; the surviving gatehouse is of *c.* 1300.

Egglestone Abbey *(English Heritage)*
1.5km S of Barnard Castle on minor road off B6277

Egglestone was among the poorest and the last of the Premonstratensian foundations, colonized in 1198 from Easby Abbey. Note the small size of Egglestone's first church, the chancel of which was subsequently much extended in a rebuilding of the later 13c. The cloister, north of the church, may have lacked a west range in the first building phase, when the community was still very small; the east range, where the canons had their chapter-house and dormitory, was converted into a private residence soon after the Dissolution, with the addition of a second storey and the insertion of new fireplaces and windows.

Fountains Abbey *(National Trust)*
3km W of Ripon off B6265 to Pateley Bridge

Wealthiest of the Cistercian houses, Fountains preserves a memorable set of buildings, unfailingly exciting to the traveller. The site is typical of the Order – a remote, well-watered valley; so successful was its first settlement that, within two decades of foundation in 1132, the great church and other buildings were extended to their present scale, filling the entire valley floor. A particularly remarkable survival from this period is the lay brothers' west range, but note also the 13c Chapel of the Nine Altars at the east end of the church and Abbot Huby's early 16c tower to the north – both contrast significantly with the deliberate austerity of the *c.* 1150 nave when the Order was still noted for its asceticism.

Franciscan (Greyfriars) Tower, Richmond
In Richmond, N of town centre

The Franciscans came to Richmond in 1258, being fifteen strong even as late as 1539, when suppressed. Urban sites like this one, not far from Richmond market, were usually redeveloped, and Richmond's tower is a rare survival of a Franciscan building. It separated the friars' choir from the large preaching nave in which they once held congregations spellbound with their eloquence.

Gisborough Priory *(English Heritage)*
In Guisborough, next to parish church

Like Bridlington, Gisborough was one of the earliest and wealthiest of the Augustinian communities, founded in 1119. It was not the luckiest, having to rebuild its church for a second time in the 13c, after a terrible fire in 1289 had destroyed what had just been completed; the surviving east end, showing no sign of economy, is of Gisborough III, the third church to stand on this site. Only the gatehouse survives of the 12c buildings; the 15c parish church, immediately to the north, was built to accommodate the lay congregation, no longer welcomed by the canons in their own nave.

Jervaulx Abbey
On A6108, 8km SE of Leyburn

Jervaulx attracts as much for its garden and arboretum as for the Cistercian ruins which are their setting – this is the perfect place for a summer afternoon. The monks first came here in 1156: their great dormitory (*c.* 1200) stands to full height still, and is the most prominent of the surviving remains. Note the meat kitchen beyond, with its three huge fireplaces: added in the Late Middle Ages, when discipline had become slack, such kitchens became familiar at many white-monk houses, extending privileges, once allowed only to the sick, to the entire self-indulgent community.

Kirkham Priory *(English Heritage)*
8km SW of Malton on minor road off A64

The founder of Kirkham in the early 1120s was Walter Espec, subsequently patron of the Cistercians at Rievaulx. It has many of the characteristics of a Cistercian house, in particular its riverine setting, and Walter himself at one time proposed to give Kirkham over to the white monks; Kirkham's Augustinians survived this threat, coming to prosper especially in the 13c as custodians of de Roos family sepulchres. To this phase of baronial patronage belong an extension of the presbytery (to hold de Roos tombs) and preparations for a complete remodelling of the claustral buildings, never more than partially carried out; surviving relics of de Roos beneficence include the very handsome late 13c laver (wash-place) in Kirkham's cloister, and a high quality gatehouse on which the family's heraldry is especially prominent.

Kirkstall Abbey
In Leeds, near Headingley station, between Abbey Road and canal bank

In this unlikely situation, on the outskirts of a sprawling industrial city, the remains of Kirkstall Abbey are, nevertheless, exceptionally complete. They include a big church and attached claustral ranges, begun in 1152 and finished, for the most part, within a generation. This is the best place in England to experience the full impact of Cistercian building at its most monumental; note the high quality of the chapter-house entrance and the comparative austerity of the other domestic buildings, many of which still stand to their full height. Kirkstall's tower, like those of other houses in the Order, was given a tall bell-stage in the early 16c, ignoring the early statute of 1157 – 'There shall be no bell-towers of stone.'

Lastingham Church
At Lastingham, on minor road 5km N of A170, 8km NW of Pickering

Lastingham's great glory is its late 11c crypt; both crypt and overlying chancel were built by migrant monks from Whitby, intending in 1078 to re-settle this ancient holy place, but removing shortly afterwards to York Abbey. Lastingham had been the monastery and burial place of the seventh-century St Cedd (d. 654), missionary bishop of the East Saxons; its post-Conquest crypt, in the Anglo-Saxon tradition, was built in the first instance as Cedd's reliquary.

Monk Bretton Priory *(English Heritage)*
1.5km E. of Barnsley town centre off A633

Monk Bretton started life in 1154 as a Cluniac house, colonized from the wealthy Pontefract Priory (*c.* 1090), with which it was later in dispute. Independent from 1281, it was described as Benedictine thereafter. The plan of Monk Bretton, which includes the foundations of both infirmary and guest-house, is unusually complete. Of special interest are the prior's lodgings on the first floor of the west claustral range (note the fine chimney-piece of his chamber), the two gatehouses, and a curious 'administrative building' in the outer court, one of very few such survivals in the country.

Mount Grace Priory *(English Heritage)*
11km NE of Northallerton on A19 near Ingleby Arncliffe

By the late 1390s, when Mount Grace was founded, Carthusians were widely viewed as a monastic élite, much admired for their exemplary self-discipline. Carthusians lived like hermits, speaking to nobody and seldom emerging from the individual cells of which there is a modern reconstruction at Mount Grace; each cell had two chambers (the lower with a food hatch into the cloister) and a tiny garden of its own. The diminutive church at Mount Grace was appropriate to a community which met seldom, which was never of great size, and which refused to share its worship with strangers.

▶Abbey sites of medieval Yorkshire which are open to the public are shown on this map. All are described in the Gazetteer.

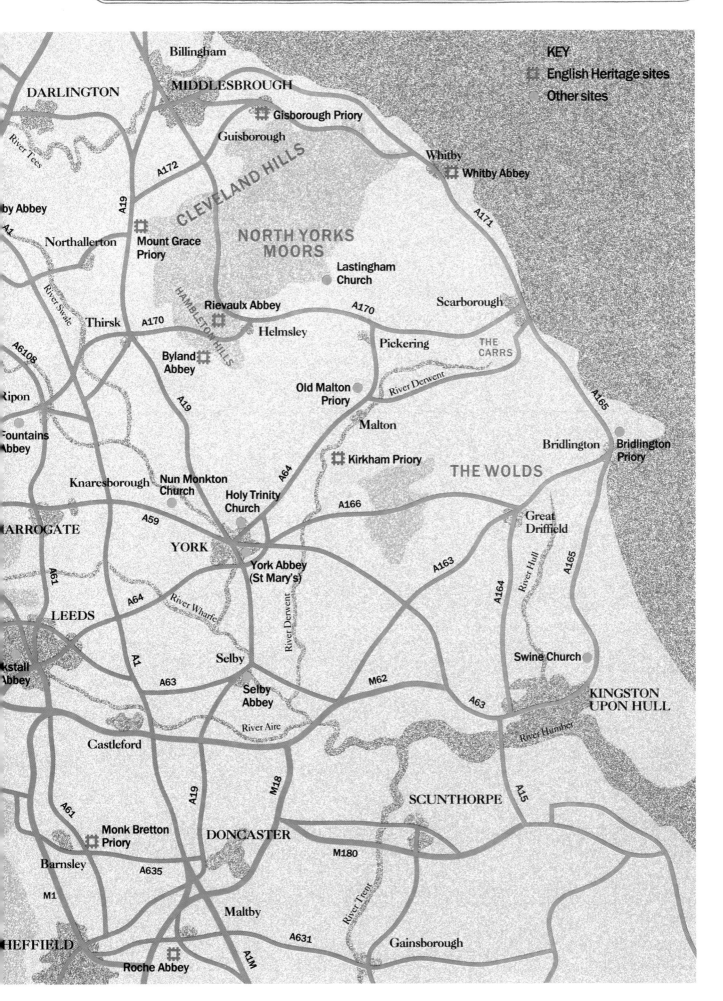

KEY

🏛 English Heritage sites
● Other sites

Billingham

DARLINGTON

MIDDLESBROUGH

🏛 Gisborough Priory

Guisborough

River Tees

A172

A19

CLEVELAND HILLS

Whitby

🏛 Whitby Abbey

A171

by Abbey

A1

Northallerton

🏛 Mount Grace Priory

NORTH YORKS MOORS

Lastingham Church

Scarborough

River Swale

Thirsk

A170

HAMBLETON HILLS

Rievaulx Abbey

A170

Helmsley

Pickering

THE CARRS

A6108

Byland Abbey

A19

River Derwent

Ripon

Old Malton Priory

Malton

A165

Fountains Abbey

Bridlington

Bridlington Priory

Knaresborough

Nun Monkton Church

🏛 Kirkham Priory

THE WOLDS

A64

Holy Trinity Church

A166

A59

Great Driffield

HARROGATE

A61

YORK

York Abbey (St Mary's)

A163

A164

River Hull

A165

A64

River Wharfe

River Derwent

LEEDS

A1

Selby

Swine Church

kstall Abbey

A63

Selby Abbey

M62

KINGSTON UPON HULL

A63

River Aire

River Humber

Castleford

A19

M18

SCUNTHORPE

A15

A61

Monk Bretton Priory

DONCASTER

M180

Barnsley

A635

M1

River Trent

Maltby

A631

Gainsborough

HEFFIELD

🏛 Roche Abbey

A1M

Nun Monkton Church
In Nun Monkton, on minor road off A59, 13km NW of York

The parish church, attractively set, is the former nave of Nun Monkton Priory, a house of Benedictine nuns; the nuns' choir was demolished at the Dissolution and there are no other significant remains of their buildings. The community was never richly endowed, yet the surviving work on the church is of high quality. It was completed in two separate campaigns, the lower part in the 1170s, the upper in the 1230s, probably on the intervention of a new patron.

Old Malton Priory
In Old Malton, 2.5km NE of Malton on A64

Malton was one of the wealthier of the Gilbertine priories, founded by St Gilbert as a 'retreat-house' for canons who, in double houses like Watton, tended communities of nuns. The canons' large church, part of which was kept for parish use at the Dissolution, is now a battered fragment, being the western part only of the former nave, lacking two of its bays to the east. A further complication internally is the *c.* 1500 work (stone panelling and other details) which followed a fire of that date; what remains is, nevertheless, a major building, very well worth stopping the car.

Rievaulx Abbey *(English Heritage)*
4km W of Helmsley on minor road off B1257

Rievaulx, colonized from St Bernard's Clairvaux in March 1132, was the Cistercians' first outpost in the North; the community recruited quickly, especially under the leadership of Abbot Ailred (1147–67). Rievaulx's great cloister is of Ailred's time, but most of the abbey's buildings are somewhat later, both the big refectory and the greatly extended presbytery being of *c.* 1200 and showing little of the austerity for which the Cistercians had earlier been renowned.

Roche Abbey *(English Heritage)*
2.5km S of Maltby off A634

The beauty of Roche is partly its setting but also the completeness of a plan which, at foundation level, exemplifies the characteristic double provision – monks to the east, lay brethren to the west – of the Cistercians. Note here, in particular, the line of the screen (*pulpitum*), three bays west of the crossing, which divided the two parts of the church. Another feature of Roche is its drainage system, still directing the swift streams which swept away the waste of communal lavatories and kitchens.

Salley Abbey *(English Heritage)*
At Sawley, 6km N of Clitheroe off A59

Salley Abbey, now within Lancashire, was the poorest of the Yorkshire Cistercian houses; even so, its foundations are impressive and would have been more so but for the late-medieval trimming-down of the community as lay brethren ceased to be recruited. At Salley, exceptionally for an English house, although common enough in contemporary Ireland, this shrinkage was accompanied by the walling-off of the nave and its abandonment; east of the crossing, the monks had more than enough room in their spacious 13c presbytery, a grand rebuilding on a much enlarged scale of the original 12c chancel.

Selby Abbey
In centre of Selby

The huge church at Selby is the only survival of a major Benedictine abbey. Its furnishings and roofs are modern, replaced after the fire of 1906; but the stonework is intact, being a textbook example of a lengthy building programme, starting with crossing and transepts of about 1110, then moving steadily westward down the nave to completion in the mid-13c. Not long afterwards, as if in love with building, Selby's monks demolished their first choir and rebuilt it in the costly Decorated style on a scale matching the nave; they had finished by 1340, just before the Black Death of 1348–9 brought their house into financial distress.

Swine Church
In Swine, on minor road off A165, 7km NE of Hull

The parish church is all that is left of a Cistercian nunnery, founded in the 1150s and originally for both nuns and canons; along with other nunneries, including the Yorkshire Sinningthwaite, Swine was refused admission to the order until after 1213, although observing Cistercian customs from much earlier. The church, which is Late Norman of *c.* 1180, was partially rebuilt in the 15c; its furnishings include pre-Dissolution choir-stalls and screens, with tombs of the Hilton family, patrons and lords of the manor.

Whitby Abbey *(English Heritage)*
On cliff top E of Whitby town centre

Whitby, as the site of St Hilda's seventh-century double monastery, was one of Yorkshire's earliest holy places. It was re-settled soon after the Conquest, in the 1070s, but preserves little of that (or any earlier) date; the ruins today are of a very grand rebuilding, begun in the 1220s and at least partly financed by the successful revival of St Hilda's cult. First to be completed was a much-enlarged, aisled presbytery; the crossing and transepts were reached in the 1250s, and are similarly Early English in style; the nave, some two generations later, is Decorated; the last modification was a Perpendicular west window, inserted during the 15c.

York Abbey (St Mary's)
In Yorkshire Museum gardens

The remains of St Mary's Abbey, which are extensive but scattered, start with a fine precinct wall, complete with towers and original gatehouses. Note the high quality, at this once rich abbey, of the late 13c work on what is left of the church, including expensive, decorative, blank arcading; other fragments, among them fine sculptures from a late 12c portal, are preserved in the Yorkshire Museum, which itself overlies claustral buildings. The former abbot's house, in the north-east corner of the twelve-acre precinct, had only recently been rebuilt when it assumed a new function, immediately after the Dissolution, as headquarters for the Council of the North; it has been in use since 1963 as teaching accommodation for the University of York.

York: Holy Trinity Priory
In Micklegate

Holy Trinity Priory was, for many years, a dependency of the French abbey at Marmoutier; it survived, most unusually, the otherwise comprehensive suppression of the 'alien priories' by Henry V in 1414, but has left few remains except in its church, taken over at the Dissolution for the parish. Here the nave arcades are 13c in date; there is some 12c work at the former crossing, but the chancel is wholly 19c.

Acknowledgements

Thanks are due to the following for permission to reproduce illustrations:
Airviews, Manchester: pages 8, 25 and 28.
Bibliothèque Municipale, Dijon: pages 9 and 16.
Bibliothèque Municipale, Douai: page 18 (MS 392, f.3r).
Bibliothèque Nationale, Paris: page 6.
Bodleian Library, Oxford: pages 2 (MS Fairfax 12, f.81r), 4 and cover (MS Bodley 39, f.1r), 18 (MS Bodley 264, f.22) and 26 (MS Auct D2.6, f.4r).
British Library: pages 4 (Arundel MS 155, f.133), 6 and cover (MS Royal 2A. XVIII, f.7v), 14 (Add. MS 39843, f.6v), 24 (Add. MS 37049, f.22v), 28 and cover (Add. MS 39943, f.39).
Cambridge University Committee for Aerial Photography: pages 5 and 34.
Durham Cathedral, Dean and Chapter Library: page 1.
Tony Marshall: page 5.
Ministry of Defence (Crown Copyright): page 32.
Musée Condé, Chantilly: page 10.
National Portrait Gallery, London: page 32.
Tate Gallery, London: page 27.
Trustees of the British Museum: page 35 (1910-2-12-282).
All other photographs © English Heritage Photography Section.